MW01288898

Whole Food

30 Days of Whole Food Cookbook:

Recipes with Life-Changing Healthy Whole Food Diet

The Ultimate Guide to Increasing Your Energy & Losing Weight

3RD Edition

EDWARDS ADAMS

ISBN-10: 1530595061
ISBN-13: 978-1530595068

CONTENTS

Foreword

I would like to thank you for purchasing 30 Days of Whole Food Cookbook: Recipes with Life-Changing Healthy Whole Food Diet to Increase Energy & Lose Weight. And congratulations on taking the much needed step towards ensuring your longevity, health, and strength in the days to come.

I've had many feedbacks and wanted to continue improving this book with more recipes and the highest quality. I appreciate it all and that is why I've created a 3rd Edition.

Through this book, you are going to discover proven steps and verified strategies on how to lose weight and gain more strength than you ever thought possible. The best part? The whole regimen is only for thirty days.

Get ready to discover awesome recipes as well as priceless tips on how to reach your desired goal: getting healthy and physically fit.

Thanks again for purchasing this book. I hope you enjoy it!

Edwards Adams

Introduction – The Realities of Obesity

Obesity has become a global epidemic with one third of the global population, or 2.1 billion, diagnosed as overweight or obese. Even children haven't been spared from this disease; the rates of obesity among this group rose by 50% between the years 1980 and 2013. Unfortunately, the burden of obesity is highest in the United States. The overweight population in the country accounts to 13% of the global obesity epidemic while China and India combined account to 15%!

What most people fail to realize is that there's more to obesity than facing a heftier version of yourself every time you look in the mirror. The extra weight they lug around is one of the prime reasons for feeling weaker and slower. Even the simple act of breathing becomes quite difficult as excess fat prevents the rib cage from expanding to its fullest and restricts the movement of the diaphragm.

Additionally, weight gain can cause health problems, such as heart disease, stroke, and diabetes. These dangerous diseases have claimed the lives of over 120,000 U.S. citizens. These deaths could have been preventable had people taken care of their diet and embraced a more active routine.

Those who survive with these diseases lead poor quality life, spending thousands monthly on medication and medical equipment like pacemakers. They're even ridden with psychological issues such as depression, which results from out-of-balance body chemistry, feelings of low self-esteem, and social isolation among other factors.

Now there are many ways that can help you shed the extra weight and lead a healthier life. However, nothing is as effective as changing the food you eat. Adding more greens, limiting carbohydrates and sugars, substituting red meats with lean meat and white meat are some changes that can help your body burn the fat it accumulated. As a result, you'll have more energy to burn, which is vital since you need to exercise and get back in shape. The biggest advantage to changing your diet though is being able to lead a happier life with the people you love.

Now time-sensitive programs to fight obesity have become popular over the past few years. These are designed to start people on a weight loss journey, showing them how great they'll look and healthy they'll feel after a specific period of time. After the followers of these programs see the results of their hard work within a relatively short period of time, they become more focused and ready to continue their efforts for a much longer time. Without a doubt, many people across the world experienced better, healthy lives by following these programs. And now it's your turn.

The following pages will introduce you to the 30-Day Whole Food program, a unique blend of recipes and valuable tips that have actually helped many people lose weight, grow strong, and enjoy better health within just 30 days. All of the information you're about to read has been thoroughly researched by both leading scientists and the humble author to ensure that you get the best results you seek.

So let's get started on our mission to make you fit, healthy, and happy with life.

.

1 Chapter 1: Introducing the 30-Day Whole Food Program

The concept of 'Whole Foods' has taken the world by storm, making the rounds in dietary circles and mentioned by nutrition experts at every opportunity. Basically, these foods are unprocessed and unrefined before their consumption or refined and processed as little as possible. This means that they won't contain salts, fats and other additives or preservatives found in some of the fattening foods most eat.

Don't confuse whole foods with organic foods though. Both are completely different since the latter are foods free of antibiotics, growth hormones, and other synthetic chemicals. They're also 'organic' since they haven't been treated with pesticides, bio-engineered, or irradiated.

By adding more whole foods to your diet, you'll get more nutrients than any supplements you've been taking. Moreover, you'll get to reap the following benefits:

- **Healthy Weight Maintenance** –Whole foods are packed with nutrition yet low on calories. Therefore, you won't have to worry about counting the calories you consume with every meal. What further makes them a great basis to any diet is that they can be used to make tantalizing dishes and desserts that will appease your palate while keeping you full for a very long time.

- **Lower Risk of Diabetes and Heart Disease** – Whole foods can help you fight heart disease as raw fruits and vegetables areas rich in fiber as whole grains if not more. Moreover, they can reduce your risk of developing type II diabetes or any ailments that result from this disease. In fact, raw vegetables and lean meat will manage your blood sugar without compromising on taste or nutritional value.

- **Cancer Prevention** – Many additives, including sugars, have been associated with the #1 killer in the world: cancer. By consuming more whole foods, you'll be able to reduce the risk of this disease and enjoy a longer, healthier life among your loved ones.

However, there's more to the 30-Day Whole Food program than just what you eat. There are three steps you should take to make the most of this program and see the results you seek.

1. **Establish a Support Network** – As in the case of any diet, you'll need people who can motivate you and ensure that you stay on track. Start looking in your family and friend circles as they are the people who can dedicate their time to you fully and maybe even join you on your weight loss through whole foods journey. If you can't find anyone, reach out to people who have embraced the whole food diet or are currently following it. You can always talk to them about your own efforts and any hardships in your way. They'll definitely give you valuable advice and even share some recipes of their own. To find such individuals, start searching online in forums, blogs, and social media.

2. **Prepare Your Home for the Whole Food Program** – Prep your home in a way that'll ensure your dedication to the plan. This means getting rid of any chocolates, chips and fattening comfort foods you have stowed away. You'll also need to clear your

cupboards of all unhealthy edibles so that you don't give up too fast. Finally, scan the rest of the house for anything that can drive you to binge on unhealthy foods and remove them at once. This includes memorabilia from your favorite fast food restaurants as these will make you yearn for their food.

3. **Start Planning Your Way to Good Health** – The 30-Day Whole Food program requires a lot of planning before you can start. This is because you need to be ready for situations that can pop up in the month ahead. For instance, your diet may force you to avoid attending a dinner party or the birthday of someone very close to you. There might even be a wedding party within that timeframe, an event you can't weasel your way out of. So, plan to ensure that nothing distracts you once you start the program.

After completing these steps, get ready to start the program. First, you'll need to stock up on the ingredients of the following 30 recipes so that you can start eating healthy and regain control of your life.

2 Chapter 2: 30 Recipes for the 30-Day Whole Food Program

A healthy diet is the basis of any program, which is why the recipes are the core subject of this book. You can try any of the following thirty recipes without worrying about your calorie count, taste, or nutritional value. Just remember to have fun while making them and ensure that the ingredients you combine are 100% fresh and free from additives.

Day 1: Recipe # 1: Thai-Inspired Meatloaf

Enjoy this flavor-filled version of the traditional meatloaf without worrying about additional inches to your waist.

Ingredients:

- Thai Relish, 6 ounces
- Thai Salsa, 16 ounces

- Beaten Eggs, 3
- Ground Beef, 2 pounds
- Ground Pork, 1 pound
- Onion, 1 (Minced)
- Cloves Garlic, 4 (Minced)
- Fresh Ginger, 2 tablespoon (Grated)
- Chili Flakes, 2 tablespoon
- Coconut Aminos, 1 ounce
- Sesame Oil, 1 ounce
- Chinese Five-spice, 1 tablespoon
- Salt & Pepper

Step-by-Step Instructions:

1. First of all, pre-heat your oven to 325°.
2. Add eggs, onion, ginger, sesame oil, salt, garlic, chili flakes, pepper, and coconut aminos in a bowl and mix everything properly.
3. At this point, mix in the Thai relish and stir all the ingredients again.
4. Shape the mixture into the form of a loaf and place the result on a sheet pan.
5. Add Thai salsa on top of the mixture and bake that for long 50 minutes.

Recipe # 2: Coconut Pancakes

Ingredients:

- 4 Eggs
- 2 Ripe Bananas
- ½ cup Coconut flour
- 3 tbsp. Coconut sugar
- 1 tbsp. Coconut oil
- 1 tsp. Baking soda
- ½ tsp. Ground cinnamon

Step-by-Step Instructions:

1. Whisk the eggs in a bowl. Add the rest of the ingredients to form a smooth batter.
2. Heat a pan and melt half coconut oil.
3. Ladle a scoopful of the mixture.
4. Cook until bubbles appear and then flip. Cook well on both sides. Serve immediately.

Day 2: Recipe # 3: Red Pepper & Noodle Stir-Fry

If you don't want to spend much time in the kitchen but can't compromise on great taste, this is just the thing.

Ingredients:

- Brooklyn Biltong, 1 cup
- Bell Peppers (red/ yellow), 3
- Yellow Onion, half
- Coconut Aminos, half cup
- Beef Broth, half cup
- Dates, two
- Garlic Cloves, two
- Grated Ginger, 1 tablespoon (fresh)
- Pepper, quarter of a tablespoon
- Olive Oil, 2 tablespoons (extra-virgin)
- Pepper
- Any kind of stir-fry vegetables according to your wish!

Step-by-Step Instructions:

1. Cut the bell peppers into strips. Make sure that the strips are thin. Next, chop the onion finely.
2. Mix the coconut aminos, dates, garlic, pepper, beef broth, and ginger until you achieve a smooth consistency.

3. Add the olive oil in a pan and let it heat for a few seconds. Sautee the onion & bell peppers for seven to ten minutes or until the vegetables become slightly tender.

Add the biltong and sauce mixture and cook for a few additional minutes.

Recipe # 4: Spicy Squash Soup

Ingredients:

- 1 (2 lb.) Butternut squash, cubed

- 2 Carrots, medium, chopped

- 1 White onion, medium, chopped

- 1 Apple, medium, chopped

- 2 tbsp. Ground cinnamon

- 1 tsp. Ground chipotle pepper

- 1 tsp. Ground cumin

- Fresh cilantro, for garnish

Step-by-Step Instructions:

1. Preheat the oven to 375 degrees F. Combine the squash, carrots, apple and onion on a large rimmed baking sheet. Sprinkle cinnamon and cumin and toss to mix together. Apple a splash of water and place it in the oven to roast. Leave it for 45 minutes.

2. Take out the veggies and place them in a large soup pot with 5 cups water and group chipotle.

3. Bring to a boil and leave to simmer until the squash is tender. Use a blender to puree the mix. Serve hot with a handful of cilantro.

Day 3: Recipe # 5: Potatoes Baked with Biltong

If you're a fan of African cuisine, you should definitely try this South African recipe and its unique twist to biltong.

Ingredients:

- Brooklyn Biltong, 3-4 pieces per potato, diced Potatoes, 2
- Ghee, 1 tablespoon
- Salt and Pepper

Step-by-Step Instructions:

1. Pre-heat the oven to 425°.
2. Wrap the potatoes in foil and cook them for around 50-60 minutes or until them seem easy to cut through with a fork.
   Split the potatoes open and add salt-pepper, ghee and the diced biltong on top.

Recipe # 6: Greek Chicken Salad

Ingredients:

- 3 cups Chicken breast, cooked and shredded

- 2 tbsp. Kalamata olives, pitted and chopped

- ¾ cup Plain yogurt

- ¾ cup Cherry tomatoes, halved

- ½ cup Mayonnaise

- 1 tsp. Fresh oregano

- 1 cup Cucumber, diced

- 3 Cloves garlic, finely chopped

- ½ cup Crumbled feta

- ¼ cup Fresh Italian parsley, chopped

Step-by-Step Instructions:

1. In a large bowl mix the yogurt, mayonnaise, garlic and oregano. Mix well until the texture is creamy.

2. Add chicken, tomato, cucumber, olives, feta and parsley and toss well.

3. Place the salad in the refrigerator for 30-60 minutes
and serve on lettuce leaves or in sandwiches.

Day 4: Recipe # 7: Biltong Eggs & Hash

A great breakfast recipe, biltong eggs and hash is the perfect way to start your day.

Ingredients:

- White Potato, 3
- Green Salsa
- Salt & Pepper
- Olive Oil, half tablespoon
- Eggs, 8
- Yellow Onion, half
- Brooklyn Biltong, 1 cup (diced)
- Cilantro

Step-by-Step Instructions:

1. Pre-heat the oven to 400° and maintain this temperature throughout.
2. Cut the potatoes into small cubes and season them with salt, olive oil and pepper.
3. Apply a baking sheet onto a baking pan and place the potatoes on top.

4. Place the pan into the oven and allow the potatoes to bake for 25-35 minutes or until they're tender. If you want them to be crispy, turn the broiler for a few minutes and watch over the potatoes lest they burn.

5. In a small ball, whisk the eggs and then add the chopped onion and diced biltong. Season with pepper and salt.

6. Add the potatoes and cook for 2-3 minutes.

7. Serve with green salsa and cilantro.

Recipe # 8: Crunchy Chicken Nuggets

Ingredients:

Cooking spray

- 1 lb. Chicken breasts, boneless, skinless, cut into 2-inch chunks

- ½ cup Plain yogurt

- 2 cups Cornflakes, crushed

- 2 tbsp. Parsley, chopped

- ½ tsp. Freshly ground white pepper

- ½ tsp. Salt

- ½ cup Honey mustard sauce for dipping

Step-by-Step Instructions:

1. Place the chicken chunks with yogurt in a medium bowl and let it marinate for an hour or overnight.

2. Preheat oven to 375 degrees F. Take a baking sheet. Grease with cooking spray.

3. Place corn flakes, parsley, salt and pepper in a large reseal able plastic bag and mix them well by shaking. Drop the chicken pieces into the bag, few pieces at a time. Seal and shake to coat and then place the chicken into the baking sheet.

4. Bake the chicken for 20-25 minutes until they are crunchy on the outside and tender in the inside.

5. Serve with honey mustard sauce for dipping.

Day 5: Recipe # 9: Marinated Mushrooms

A great snack, side dish or light supper, marinated mushrooms will definitely make everyone at home want to join your 30-Day Whole Food program.

Ingredients:

- Red-wine Vinegar, half cup
- Olive Oil, 6 tablespoon, (extra-virgin)
- Sea Salt or Kosher Salt, 1 tablespoon
- Dried Oregano, 1 tablespoon
- Fresh Ground Pepper, half tablespoon
- Garlic Cloves, 3 (minced)
- Fresh Parsley, 2 tablespoon (chopped)
- Button Mushrooms, 2 pounds (preferably fresh and small sized)

Step-by-Step Instructions

1. Clean the mushrooms then start cooking them in hot water with salt mixed in. Drain the mushrooms once they become tender and place them in a bowl.
2. Combine all the ingredients aside from parsley in a bowl. Whisk them thoroughly before pouring the mixture over the mushrooms.
3. Toss the mushrooms to coat them with the mixture and then allow them to soak it in the fridge for at least two hours.
4. Add the chopped parsley before serving the mushrooms and toss them one last time to cover them with parsley.

Recipe # 10: Black Pepper Roast Beef with a Honey Glaze

Ingredients:

- 1 (4 lbs.) Beef top round roast

- 2 tbsp. Black pepper, coarsely ground

- 1 tbsp. Coarse sea salt

- 6 tbsp. Honey

- 3 tbsp. Balsamic vinegar

- 1 tbsp. Canola oil, expeller-pressed

Step-by-Step Instructions:

1. Preheat the oven to 400 degrees F. Rub salt and pepper all over the beef. Place the beef on a rack fitted into roasting pan. Roast for 45 minutes.

2. In a medium bowl, whisk together honey, vinegar, and oil. After 45 minutes of roasting beef, use a brush and apply the honey mixture all over the beef. Cook for 15 more minutes, and then reduce oven temp to 350 degrees.

3. Insert a thermometer in the beef to check if the thick part reads 125 degrees for medium rare. Keep brushing with honey glaze every 15 minutes and roast some more.

4. Place the roast on the cutting board, tent with a foil and let it rest for 15 minutes before slicing. This increases internal temp by 5 to 10 degrees.

5. Serve with the pan juices drizzled over top.

Day 6: Recipe # 11: Slow Cooker Cauliflower Mash

If you don't like cauliflower, this recipe will change your mind and make you wonder why you've avoided eating this dish for so long.

Ingredients:

- Head Cauliflower, 1 (chopped)
- Garlic Cloves, 2 (finely chopped)
- Salt or Himalayan Salt, half teaspoon
- Ground Pepper, quarter of a teaspoon (fresh)
- Bay leaf, one
- Olive Oil, 2 teaspoons, (extra-virgin)
- Fresh Herbs, 2 teaspoons (chopped)
- Pepitas, 2 teaspoons (optional)

Step-by-Step Instructions

1. In a slow cooker, place all the ingredients except for fresh herbs, pepitas and olive oil). Fill the cooker with enough to cover the cauliflower and add the lid to begin cooking.
2. On a low flame, let the vegetable cook for six hours.
3. Strain the cauliflower and throw away the bay leaf.
4. Add some oil and a bit of salt and pepper to the mix.
5. Using a potato masher, mash everything until you achieve the consistency you want.
6. Taste the mix and add salt or pepper if necessary. Use fresh herbs and pepitas for garnishing and serve.

Recipe # 12: Fish Fingers

Ingredients:

- 2 lbs. Cod fillets

- 2 ½ cups Breadcrumbs (gluten-free)

- ¼ cup Rice milk

- 1 tsp. Garlic powder

- ¼ tsp. Paprika powder

- ½ tsp. Onion powder

- Salt and pepper to taste

- Olive oil for frying

Step-by-Step Instructions:

1. Marinate the fillets with milk, onion powder, garlic powder, paprika, salt and pepper for a few hours.

2. Once done, roll the fish fillets into the breadcrumbs.

3. Heat oil in a pan and deep fry the fish fillets. Don't overcrowd the pan.

4. Serve hot with a dip you wish.

Day 7: Recipe # 13: Avocado & Prosciutto Stuffed-Mushrooms

Another delicious mushroom-based recipe, this one is quite filling despite the dainty pieces covering your plate.

Ingredients :

- Prosciutto, two to three pieces
- Baby bella-mushrooms, 8 pounds (stems removed)
- Olive Oil, one tablespoon
- Avocado, 1 (preferably large)
- Baby Spinach (half cup)
- Lemon Juice, 1 tablespoon (fresh)
- Basil Leaves, 1 tablespoon (fresh)
- Parsley Leaves, 1 tablespoon (fresh)
- Garlic Cloves, half cup
- Onion Powder, 2 tablespoons
- Himalayan Salt or Sea Salt, 1/8 teaspoon
- Pepper, quarter of a teaspoon

Step-by-Step Instructions:

1. Preheat the oven to 420°.
2. Use foil paper or parchment paper to line two baking sheets.
3. Fold the prosciutto pieces, place them on the baking sheet, and put the latter inside the oven. Cook them for five minutes and then flip them to bake the other side for another five.
4. If you want your prosciutto to be crispy, broil for one more minute. Take the sheet out and let its contents cool down.

5. After removing the mushroom stems, run them under cool water to rinse them and finally dry them with a paper towel.

6. On the second lined baking sheet, place the mushrooms and coat them thoroughly with olive oil. You can also sprinkle salt on each mushroom.

7. Cook the mushrooms at 425° for around five to six minutes. After removing the mushrooms from the oven, drain them and pat them dry with a paper towel. Set them aside to cool.

8. Slice the avocado and place it in your blender with baby spinach, parsley, lemon juice, garlic, basil leaves, salt, pepper, and onion powder. Stop blending once you get a smooth mixture.

9. Scoop the avocado mixture into each mushroom and sprinkle crumbled prosciutto pieces over it. Use parsley to garnish and serve.

Recipe # 14: Veggies and Tofu Stir Fry

Ingredients:

- 1 ½ cup Cooked brown rice

- 14 oz. Extra firm tofu

- 2 cups Carrots, shredded

- 1 cup Bell peppers, sliced

- 1 cup Asparagus, chopped

- ½ cup packed Kale

- 2 minced Garlic cloves

- 2 tbsp. Olive oil

- Salt and pepper to taste

Step-by-Step Instructions:

1. Heat oil in a pan and fry garlic until golden. Add the tofu and stir-fry until golden brown.

2. Add the veggies and fry until they are tender but intact.

3. Season well and serve with brown rice.

Day 8: Recipe # 15: Beet, Orange & Fennel Salad with Radicchio

Don't get bored with the usual salad. Try this recipe to discover a flavor filled healthy option.

Ingredients:

- Beets, 4 (peeled and rinsed)
- Olive Oil, 2 tablespoons
- Oranges, 3 (preferably blood oranges)
- Fennel Bulb, 1
- Red Onion, quarter
- Radicchio, one head
- Parsley, half cup (chopped)
- Cilantro, one-third of a cup (chopped)
- Orange Vinegar, 1 tablespoon
- Lemon, half
- Lime, half
- Olive Oil, one tablespoon
- Pepper
- Sea Salt

Step-by-Step Instructions:

1. Place the beets in a square piece of foil. Use olive oil to coat the vegetable lightly and then fold the foil around it. Roast at 350° for 45 minutes or until the beets can be pierced easily with a fork.
2. Once done, remove the beets from the oven and allow them to cool down for at least ten minutes. Don't wait long though as you need the beets warm for the upcoming steps.
3. Slice the beets and place them in a bowl.
4. Peel and roughly chop the oranges into bite sized pieces. Add them to the beets.
5. Slice the fennel bulb with a mandolin or a chef's knife to ensure thin slices. Add the slices to the bowl.
6. Chop the radicchio, parsley and cilantro before mixing them with the rest of the vegetables and oranges.
7. Drizzle the blend with vinegar, lime juice, olive oil and lemon juice. Toss everything lightly to coat the salad and add sea salt and black-pepper.
8. Wait for an hour before serving the salad so that the contents can settle.

Recipe # 16: Rosemary Lamb Chops

Ingredients:

- 6 Lamb chops

- 2 Garlic cloves, minced

- 2 tbsp. Lemon juice

- 3 tbsp. Fresh rosemary, chopped

- Salt and pepper to taste

- 2 tbsp. Olive oil

Step-by-Step Instructions:

1. Marinate the lamb chops with seasonings for a few hours.

2. Preheat the oven to 350 degrees F.

3. Grease baking pan and place the lamb on them. Bake for 30 minutes to 45 minutes.

4. Flip the chops halfway through baking process.

5. Serve hot.

Day 9: Recipe # 17: Herbed Almond-Salad

If your salad requires a little crunch, this recipe will do just that. In addition to a great taste, you'll get a wonderful energy boost.

Ingredients :

- Soaked Almonds, one handful
- Fresh Mint, one bundle (stems removed)
- Fresh Parsley, two bundles (stems removed)
- Purple Onion, half
- Tomatoes, 2 (medium sized)
- Small cucumbers, two (peeled)
- Olive Oil, quarter cup
- Lemon Juice, 2 tablespoons
- Fresh black pepper (milled)

Step-by-Step Instructions:

1. Soak the almonds in water for at least eight hours.
2. Drain the almonds and blanch them for 30 seconds in boiling water.
3. Transfer the blanched almonds in a bowl filled with ice water. After one minute, remove the skins of the almonds and crush them in a food processor until coarsely crumbled.

4. Chop the mint, parsley, tomatoes and onions. Mix in lemon juice and olive oil.

5. Add the chopped almonds and toss the salad with dressing. Add fresh ground black pepper.

Recipe # 18: Chicken and Cabbage Salad

Ingredients:

- 1 Chicken breast, cooked and cubed

- 2 cups Cabbage, sliced

- 2 tbsp. Cilantro, chopped

- ½ tbsp. Ginger shredded finely, browned

- ½ tbsp. Garlic, minced finely, chopped

- 1 tbsp. Rice vinegar

- 1 tbsp. Olive oil

- Salt and pepper to taste

Step-by-Step Instructions:

1. Toss all the ingredients together in a large bowl.

2. Serve.

Day 10: Recipe # 19: Gremolata

If you're up for Italian cuisine, try this recipe. To further make it wholly nutritious, you can add Pecorino Romano cheese, anchovy, or pine nuts.

Ingredients

- Lemon Zest, half tablespoon
- Orange Zest, half tablespoon
- Italian Parsley, three tablespoons (finely chopped)
- Basil, 3 tablespoons (properly chopped)
- Garlic Cloves, 4
- Capers, 1 tablespoon
- Pine Nuts, 3 tablespoons (toasted)
- Red-pepper flakes, 1 tablespoon
- Finishing Oil such as Olive Oil, Avocado etc. (drizzled in amount)
- Steamed Vegetables (asparagus, green beans or broccoli)

Step-by-Step Instructions:

1. Start by mincing the garlic.

2. In a pan, toast the pine nuts until they're slightly golden.

3. Combine all the ingredients in a small bowl.

4. Drizzle a tiny amount of finishing oil over the mixture and toss it.

5. Add the steamed vegetables to the gremolata and toss everything one last time.

Recipe # 20: Lentil Chili

__Ingredients:__

- 2 ¼ cups Brown lentils

- 3 cups Diced tomatoes

- 8 cups Low-sodium vegetable broth, divided

- 2 tbsp. Olive oil

- 1 Yellow onion, medium, chopped

- 1 Red bell pepper, large, chopped

- 5 Garlic cloves, finely chopped

- 4 tsp. Salt-free chili powder

- ¼ cup Fresh cilantro, chopped

Step-by-Step Instructions:

1. Heat a large pot. Put the oil and add onion, bell pepper and cook until the veggies turn brown and begin to stick to the bottom. Stir in about 3 tablespoons of broth and continue to cook until onion are soft and slightly browned.

2. Add the garlic and chili powder and stir constantly.

3. Add lentils, tomatoes and the rest of the broth. Boil the mix and reduce heat and simmer for 30 minutes until lentils are tender.

4. Uncover and cook for 30 minutes more. Stir in cilantro and serve.

Day 11: Recipe # 21: Grilled Salmon with Avocado Salsa

Looking for a delicious, easy AND healthy recipe? Try this one to enjoy a burst of flavors with each bite.

Ingredients:

- Salmon, 2 pounds (cut in four pieces)
- Olive Oil, 1 tablespoon (Extra Virgin)
- Salt, 1 tablespoon
- Ground Cumin, 1 teaspoon
- Paprika Powder, 1 teaspoon
- Onion Powder, 1 teaspoon
- Ancho Chili Powder, half teaspoon
- Black Pepper, half teaspoon
- Avocado, 1 (sliced)
- Cilantro, 2 tablespoons (chopped)
- Juice from Two Limes

Step-by-Step Instructions:

1. Rub the salmon filets with a combination of salt, chili powder, paprika, cumin, onion powder, and black

pepper mixed with olive oil. Refrigerate the filets for at least 30 minutes.

2. Pre-heat the grill while you prepare the avocado salsa. For the latter, add the avocado, onion, lime juice, cilantro, and salt (as much as you need) in a bowl. Mix the content well and allow them to chill in the fridge until you need to use them.

3. Grill the salmon until desired doneness. Add the avocado salsa on top and serve.

Recipe # 22: Shrimp and Mango Ceviche

Ingredients:

- ¾ lbs. Shrimps, medium, peeled and deveined

- 1 Mango, large, peeled, pitted and chopped

- ½ cup Red onion, finely chopped

- ¼ cup Cilantro, roughly chopped

- 6 tbsp. Lime juice

- 1 Tomato, chopped

- 1 Jalapeño pepper, seeded and finely chopped

- ¾ tsp. Fine sea salt

Step-by-Step Instructions:

1. Bring a pot of water, generously salted, to a boil. Add the shrimps and cook for about a minute or 2, until they are pink and done. Drain and rinse under cold water. Drain excess water.

2. Chop the shrimps into ½ inch pieces. Place them in a large bowl and add onion, cilantro, lime juice, tomato, mango, jalapeño, and salt. Toss well, Cover and refrigerate for an hour. Serve cold.

Day 12: Recipe # 23: Sweet Potato Fritters

Sweet potatoes can easily appease your sweet tooth's cravings in a healthy way. Just remember to not prepare too much of this batch or else you'll end up overeating, a problem that goes against all your weight loss efforts.

Ingredients:

- Sweet Potatoes, 2 cups (shredded with a cheese grater)
- Scallions or Onions, 3 (chopped)
- Eggs, 3
- Coconut Flour, quarter of a cup
- Arrowroot Starch, 2 tablespoons
- Sea Salt, 1 teaspoon
- Black Pepper, half teaspoon
- Onion Powder, half teaspoon
- Ghee, quarter cup

Step-by-Step Instructions:

1. Pre-heat the frying pan on a medium flame.

2. Beat the eggs in a large mixing ball and add the sweet potato shreds and chopped scallions or onions. Mix everything lightly.

3. Combine the coconut flour, salt, black pepper, onion powder, and arrowroot. Add these into the large bowl and mix everything.

4. Start heating the ghee. In the meanwhile, make eight balls of this batter and flatten them before placing them on the pan.

5. Fry each side for three to four minutes or until they're brown and crisp.

Recipe # 24: Chickpea and Spinach Omelette

Ingredients:

- 2 cups Chickpea flour

- 3 cups Baby Spinach

- ½ cup Yeast

- 2 tbsp. Flaxseeds

- 2 tsp. Turmeric

- 2 tsp. Baking soda

- 1 tsp. Garlic powder

- Salt to taste

Step-by-Step Instructions:

1. Cut the spinach finely and set aside.

2. In a large bowl, mix all the ingredients together (except spinach) and add a little water.

3. Make a smooth batter which is neither too thick nor too runny. Add the spinach to the mix.

4. Heat a non-stick pan and ladle a scoop of batter. Wait till one side become done. Then flip it over. Cook until done and serve immediately.

Day 13: Recipe # 25: Buffalo Chicken Sliders

Chicken lovers will love this recipe, especially since it's a great alternative to burgers. Try this recipe and combine it with sweet potato fritters for a fancy meal.

Ingredients :

- Chicken, 1 pound (ground)

- Celery, half cup (chopped)
- Carrot, half cup (shredded)
- Scallion or Green Onion, quarter cup (chopped)
- Hot Sauce, quarter cup (read the label to ensure no additives)
- Garlic, 1 teaspoon (granulated)
- Onion Powder, 1 teaspoon
- Sea Salt, 1 teaspoon
- Pepper, half teaspoon

Step-by-Step Instructions:

1. Mix all the ingredients in a large bowl.
2. Form as many patties as possible.
3. Grill the patties or fry them in ghee.

Recipe # 26: Thai Shrimp and Carrot Salad

Ingredients:

- 8 oz. Uncooked brown rice noodles

- ½ pound peeled, deveined and cooked medium shrimps (tails removed)

- ¼ cup Lime juice

- ¼ cup Rice vinegar

- 3 cups Shredded carrots

- 1/8 tbsp. Red chili pepper (crushed)

- ½ cup Unsalted peanuts (dry roasted)

- ½ cups Shallots (sliced)

- ½ cup Fresh mint (chopped)

Step-by-Step Instructions:

1. Cook noodles as per the instructions in the package. Rinse, cool, drain and place in large bowl.

2. In another bowl, mix the lime juice, vinegar and crushed pepper to make the dressing. Toss 2 tablespoons of it on the noodles and mix.

3. The remaining dressing can be used with the shrimp, shallots, carrots, peanuts and mint. Serve this shrimp mixture over the rice noodles.

Day 14: Recipe # 27: Oven-Braised Mexican Beef

Enjoy this recipe made from whole foods and revel in its Mexican twist to

forget ever ordering takeout.

Ingredients :

- Boneless Beef Short Ribs, Brisket or Stew Meat, 2.5 pounds
- Chili Powder, 1 tablespoon
- Kosher Salt, 1.5 tablespoons
- Ghee, 1 tablespoon
- Onion, 1 (thinly sliced)
- Tomato Paste, 1 tablespoon
- Garlic Cloves, 6 (peeled and crushed)
- Roasted Salsa, half cup (read its label)
- Chicken Stock, half cup
- Red Boat Fish Sauce, half teaspoon
- Cilantro, half cup (minced; optional)
- Radishes, two (thinly sliced; optional)

Step-by-Step Instructions:

1. Pre-heat the oven to 300°.
2. Combine the beef with chili powder and salt in a large bowl.
3. Heat the ghee in a large Dutch oven over medium heat. Add onions and sauté them until they become translucent.
4. Stir in tomato paste and fry for 30 seconds.
5. Toss in the garlic and beef and sauté for a minute. Pour salsa, stock and fish sauce on them.
6. Once the mixture starts boiling, cover the pot and place the pot in the oven for three hours or until the beef is tender.
7. Serve with cilantro and radishes as garnishing.

Recipe # 28: Roasted Brussel Sprouts with Bacon and Walnuts

Ingredients:

- 3 slices Thick-cut bacon, sliced into 1/2-inch wide strips

- 2 lbs. Brussels sprouts, halved

- ½ cup Walnuts, toasted and chopped

- ¼ tsp Ground black pepper

- ¼ tsp. Fine sea salt

- 1 tsp. Fresh thyme, chopped

Step-by-Step Instructions:

1. Preheat the oven to 400°F.

2. In an oven-proof skillet, cook the bacon until they are crispy. Move the bacon to the paper towel lined plate.

3. In the same skillet, add the sprouts, salt and pepper and toss till you combine them. Then place the skillet in the oven and roast the sprouts until they are deep golden brown, crispy outside and cooked inside. Stir occasionally.

4. Move the sprouts to a serving dish and toss in the bacon, walnuts and thyme. Serve.

Day 15: Recipe # 29: Cajun Crab Cakes

If you're up for a savory dish that's just the right amount of spicy, this is the one. Get ready to transport to Louisiana with this southern style recipe.

Ingredients:

- Lump Crab Cake, 1 pound
- Mayonnaise, 3 tablespoons
- Lemon Juice, 1 teaspoon
- Fresh Dill, 1.5 tablespoon
- Egg, 1
- Onion Powder, quarter teaspoon
- Garlic Powder, quarter teaspoon
- Cayenne Pepper, quarter teaspoon
- Paprika, half teaspoon
- Salt, half teaspoon
- Black Pepper, pinch
- Almond Flour, one third cup
- Red Pepper, one forth (finely chopped)

For the Remoulade Sauce

- Red Pepper, remaining three quarters
- Green Onion Stalk, 1
- Coconut Cream, three quarters of a cup
- Dijon Mustard, 2 tablespoons
- Ketchup, 3 tablespoons
- Worcestershire Sauce, half teaspoon

- Paprika, 1 teaspoon
- Cayenne, pinch
- Salt, half teaspoon
- Flat Parsley Leaves, half tablespoon

Step-by-Step Instructions:

1. Pre-heat the oven to 400°. Next, grease the surface of the baking sheet or use a baking liner.
2. Drain the crabmeat and pat it dry with a paper towel.
3. Whisk the mayonnaise, dill, egg, lemon juice, and seasoning. Fold this mixture on top of the crabmeat until well combined.
4. Sprinkle the almond flour over the mixture and then fold. Repeat this step two more times. Fold in the red pepper and the refrigerate between half an hour and three hours.
5. Make six cakes on top of the baking sheet and slip the latter into the oven for 20 to 25 minutes.
6. While the cakes cook, place all the ingredients of the sauce in your blender and puree until smooth.

Recipe # 30: Chicken Sausage with Cauliflower and Red Lentils

Ingredients:

- 1 tbsp. Canola oil

- 1 (12 oz.) pack of Cilantro chicken sausage, cooked and sliced

- 1 cup Red lentils, rinsed and drained

- 1 (16 oz.) pack of Frozen cauliflower, defrosted and drained

- 1 tbsp. Brown mustard seeds

- 2 cups Low-sodium chicken broth

- 1 ¾ cups Fresh tomatoes (chopped)

- 1 tsp. Fine sea salt

Step-by-Step Instructions:

1. Heat oil in a large pan and add the sausage and cook until browned. Stir occasionally. Transfer to plate and set aside.

2. Now place the pan over heat and add mustard seeds and toast for 30 seconds. Add broth and scrape any brown bits.

3. Then add the cauliflowers and lentils and bring to a boil. Reduce heat to medium-low, cover and let simmer until the liquid is absorbed.

4. Add the tomatoes and simmer until mixture is creamy and lentils are tender.

5. Add salt to taste. Toss in the browned sausage and serve.

Day 16: Recipe # 31: Cabbage Enchiladas

Enchiladas are quite easy to make and flexible enough to accommodate whatever ingredients you deem fit. By using cabbages as wraps instead of the usual options, you're going to feel full without consuming too many calories or gaining more weight.

Ingredients :

- Ground Beef, 1 pound
- Cumin, 1 teaspoon
- Chili Powder, 1 teaspoon
- Onion, 1
- Garlic Clove, 1
- Stir Fry Vegetable Mix, 2 cups
- Mushrooms, 10
- Ghee

Step-by-Step Instructions;

1. Cook the beef with all the ingredients mentioned above. Once done, set it aside to cool.

2. Hold a head of cabbage and make a cut at the bottom of the leaf. Wash the cabbage under running water and wait a few seconds to peel the leaf easily.

3. Place water in a pan, add salt, and bring the pan's contents to a boil. Cook the leaves for a few minutes.

4. Pre-heat the oven to 350° and fill the leaves with the mix. Roll them up and bake them for 20 minutes.

Recipe # 32: Devilled Eggs with Avocado-Lime

Ingredients:

- 3 hard-boiled eggs

- ½ Ripe avocado

- ½ Lime

- 1 tsp. Sriracha/any hot sauce

- Dash of chipotle seasoning

- Dash of celery salt

- Salt and pepper to taste

Step-by-Step Instructions:

1. Peel the eggs and slice them lengthwise

2. Remove the yolks and place in a bowl with sliced avocado. Smash them both to make a smooth paste.

3. Add the juice of the lime, hot sauce, chipotle seasoning and celery salt and mix well. Season with salt and pepper.

4. Spoon the yolk mixture back into the egg halves.

5. Serve with a sprinkle of chipotle.

Day 17: Recipe # 33: Ginger Chicken

Ginger is one of the best spices to use in cooking. Not only does it produce a strong taste and smell, it makes your food healthier. Here's a Filipino recipe that combines this spice with chicken for a great taste.

Ingredients

- Chicken Drumsticks, 1.25 pounds
- Yellow Onion, 1 (diced)
- Ginger, 1 (fresh, peeled and sliced)
- Sea Salt, half teaspoon
- Red Onion, 2 tablespoons (diced)
- Green Onion, 1 stalk (chopped)
- Ghee, 1 tablespoon
- Black Pepper, half teaspoon (optional)

Step-by-Step Instructions:

1. Add the ghee in a skillet and place it over a medium flame. Add the onion and ginger and cook them for three minutes.

2. Place the drumsticks in the skillet and add the seasonings. Cover the skillet and turn the heat to low. Allow the chicken to cook for 35 to 40 minutes.
3. Add the red onion to the gingery sauce which the chicken gravy created. Cook for three minutes.
4. If you want the chicken to be crispy, remove it from the skillet and broil it for three to five minutes before returning it from the pan.
5. Serve with chopped green onion as garnish.

Recipe # 34: Egg and Salmon Canapé

Ingredients:

- 4 Gluten free crackers

- 4 pieces Smoked salmon

- 1 Hard-boiled egg, chopped

- 2 tbsp. Coconut cream

- 1 tbsp. Chives, chopped

- 1 tbsp. Parsley, chopped

- Salt and pepper to taste

Step-by-Step Instructions:

1. In a bowl, mix the egg, coconut cream, parsley, chives, salt and pepper.

2. On each cracker place this mixture along with a smoked salmon piece on top.

3. Serve immediately.

Day 18: Recipe # 35: 5-Spice Slow Cooker Pork Ribs

Most Asian recipes use whole foods, including this recipe. All you need to do is place the ingredients and let the slow cooker.

Ingredients:

- St. Louis Pork Ribs or Baby Back, 3 to 4 pounds
- Chinese Five-Spice Powder, 2 teaspoons
- Garlic Powder, three quarter teaspoon (granulated)
- Jalapeño, 1 (fresh; cut in rings)
- Rice Vinegar, 2 tablespoons
- Coconut Aminos, 2 tablespoons
- Tomato Paste, 1 tablespoon
- Salt and Black Pepper

Step-by-Step Instructions:

1. Cut the ribs in such a way that the pieces can fit vertically in the slow cooker. Sprinkle the ribs generously with salt and pepper.

2. In a small bowl, mix the five-spice and garlic powder. Massage the mixture onto the meat to coat it.

3. In the slow cooker, first add the jalapeño rings followed by the rice vinegar, coconut aminos, and tomato paste. Stir the liquids well before adding the ribs standing up. You can use a roasting rack to ensure that the meat doesn't lie on the bottom in the liquid.

4. Cover the cooker and cook for six hours on high or eight to ten hours on low.

5. Once the ribs are quite tender, remove them from the cooker. Place the liquid in a container and refrigerate until the fat separates from the liquid. Remove the fat and boil the rest of the content. Simmer for a few minutes and use the sauce to drizzle the meet.

6. To make the ribs crispy, place them in the oven to cook for ten minutes at 400°.

Recipe # 36: Burritos

Ingredients:

- 3 Baked potatoes, cubed

- 4-6 Whole wheat tortillas

- 1 Sweet onion, chopped

- 1 Red pepper, chopped

- ½ Bunch kale, chopped

- 1 tbsp. Olive oil

- Avocado, sliced

- Tofutti cream and fresh salsa for dressing

- Salt to taste

Step-by-Step Instructions:

1. Heat oil in a pan. Add the onions and pepper and cook them for few minutes. Then add the baked potatoes and cook until they are crispy. Add salt to taste.

2. Remove pan from flame. Add the chopped kale to the cooked veggies and cover the lid for 2-3 minutes. This will steam the kale.

3. Use another pan and heat the tortillas on both sides. Scoop the veggies in the middle of the tortillas and top with Tofutti cream, avocado and fresh salsa. Serve.

Day 19: Recipe # 37: Rotisserie Chicken

Make your own rotisserie chicken without worrying about unhealthy additives. The following recipe has the potential to become a household favorite.

Ingredients :

- Whole Chicken, 4-5 pounds
- Olive Oil, 2 tablespoons (extra virgin)
- Dried Thyme, 1 teaspoon
- Garlic Powder, 1 teaspoon
- Sea Salt, 1 teaspoon
- Paprika, 1 teaspoon
- Ground Black Pepper, 1 teaspoon
- Cayenne Pepper, half teaspoon (optional)

Step-by-Step Instructions:

1. Rinse and pat the chicken dry.

2. Line your slow cooker with six balls of aluminum foil or use a roasting rack to keep the vegetables elevated while cooking.

3. Combine the dry spices in a small bowl and then add the olive oil. Season the chicken with this mixture and ensure that it's thoroughly coated.

4. Place the chicken on top of the vegetables and cook on a low flame for six to eight hours or until the chicken is cooked thoroughly.

5. To make the chicken skin crispy and brown, broil it in the oven for five to ten minutes.

Recipe # 38: Turkey Sausages

Ingredients:

- 1 ½ lb. Ground turkey

- 2 Apples, medium, peeled and grated. Squeeze out the excess liquid.

- 2 Eggs, beaten

- ½ cup Parsley, chopped

- 3 tbsp. Fresh sage, finely chopped

- ½ tsp. Ground nutmeg

- ½ tsp. Ground black pepper

- 1 ½ tsp. Salt

Step-by-Step Instructions:

1. Preheat the oven to 350 degrees F.

2. Mix the turkey, apples, eggs, parsley, sage, nutmeg, salt and pepper in a large bowl.

3. With a damp hand, shape the sausage mixture to make 8 patties.

4. In a non-stick skillet, brush some oil and heat.

5. Place the patties and brown them. Place the browned patties to the baking sheet and bake in the oven for 10 minutes until they are cooked through.

6. Serve.

Day 20: Recipe # 39: Garlic Olive Shrimp and Zucchini Noodles

Whether you want to celebrate summer or need to remind yourself of it during winter, this is the perfect, refreshing recipe to get this job done.

Ingredients :

- Zucchini, 4 cups (spiralized)
- Fresh Shrimp, half a pound
- Olive Oil, half cup (extra virgin)
- Green Olives, half cup (pitted)
- Chopped Parsley, half cup
- Garlic Cloves, 3
- Juice of Half a Lemon
- Salt

Step-by-Step Instructions:

1. Heat the oil in a sauté pan. Add the garlic and sauté it over a low-medium flame.
2. Once the garlic becomes fragrant, add the shrimp. Sauté the shrimp until it becomes slightly pink.
3. Add the zucchini noodles, olives and lemon juice. Cook everything for five minutes or until the noodles are soft.
4. Top with fresh parsley and serve.

Recipe # 40: Coconut Pumpkin Butter with Toast

Ingredients:

- 1 cup Pumpkin puree

- 1 cup Coconut butter

- 3 tbsp. Maple syrup

- 1 ½ tsp. Cinnamon (ground)

- 1/8 Nutmeg (ground)

- Salt to taste

- 4 Gluten free toasts

Step-by-Step Instructions:

1. . Combine all the ingredient together and mix well.

2. Spread the mix on a gluten free toast. Serve.

3. The mix can be refrigerated for a week as well.

Day 21: Recipe # 41: Monkey Salad

No, monkey meat isn't a whole food! This unique five-minute salad offers a healthy blend of assorted fruits, nuts, seeds and coconut flakes that will make you overflow with energy.

Ingredients:

- Banana, 1 (peeled and sliced)
- Coconut Chips, a handful
- Cashews, a handful (roasted and unsalted)
- Berries, half a cup (optional)

Step-by-Step Instructions:

1. Mix everything together and serve right away.

Recipe # 42: Mixed Grilled Vegetables

Ingredients:

- ½ cup Sweet bell peppers, quartered

- ½ cup Hot peppers, whole or cut in half

- ½ cup Zucchini and summer squash, cut into small planks

- ½ cup Mushrooms, whole/sliced

- ½ cup Onions, sliced

- 2 Tomatoes, whole

- ½ cup Corn, cleaned and cut or whole

- 1 Lime juice

Step-by-Step Instructions:

1. Prepare the vegetables and then brush them with olive oil.

2. Cook them on a clean hot grill until they are crisp and tender for about 8-10 minutes.

3. Serve hot with a sprinkle of lime juice.

Day 22: Recipe # 43: Slow Cooker Beef Curry

Curry is one of the simplest recipes you can make, especially if you want to treat yourself but don't have much time on your hands. This is the easiest recipe you'll fine to prepare this dish, so save it for the future.

Ingredients

- Beef Stew Meat or Chuck Roast, 2-3 pounds
- Homemade Coconut Milk
- Red Curry Paste, 3 tablespoons

For Coconut Milk

- Finely Shredded Coconut, 8 ounces
- Hot Water, 4 cups (not boiling)

Step-by-Step Instructions:

1. Start by preparing the homemade coconut milk. First, blend the coconut and hot water for 45 seconds in your food processor. Empty the liquid in a nut milk bag (or strainer lined with two layers of cheesecloth) and collect the strained liquid in a large bowl. Refrigerate it until use.

2. Add beef, coconut milk and curry paste in your slow cooker. Make sure to mix the curry paste well before cooking the meat for six to eight hours.

3. Pull apart the beef using two forks and then remove it from the liquid.

Recipe # 44: Salsa Halibut

Ingredients:

- 4 Halibut fillets

- 1 tbsp. Olive oil

- 2 Tomatoes, diced

- 2 Garlic cloves, minced

- 1 tsp. Fresh oregano, chopped

- 2 tbsp. Fresh basil, chopped

Step-by-Step Instructions:

1. In a bowl, combine the olive oil, oregano, garlic and basil.

2. Coat all the fillets with this mixture.

3. Place the fillets on a baking sheet that's pre-oiled and pour the diced tomatoes on top.

4. Bake for 10-15 minutes at 350 degrees F.

5. Serve with a dip of your choice.

Day 23: Recipe # 45: Spinach Sausage Scramble

An ideal breakfast recipe that can double as a light dinner, spinach sausage scramble will easily be your favorite dish during the 30-Day Whole Food program.

Ingredients :

- Chicken Sausage, 1 link (cooked and ground)
- Fresh Spinach, half cup (chopped)
- Eggs, 2 (beaten)
- Yellow Onion, one quarter (chopped)
- Olive Oil, 1 tablespoon
- Salt, Black Pepper and Garlic Powder

Step-by-Step Instructions:

1. Heat the olive oil in a sauté pan before adding the onion and sausage.
2. Once the onion becomes translucent, add the spinach. Cook until the spinach grows limp. If you want, you can add the salt, black pepper and garlic powder for taste.

3. Pour the eggs and scramble them over the spinach and sausage. Serve once the eggs are lightly scrambled.

Recipe # 46: Easy Garlic Green Beans

Ingredients:

- 2 cups Frozen green beans

- 1 tbsp. Olive oil

- 1 tsp. Chopped garlic

- 1/4 cup water

- Salt and pepper to taste

Step-by-Step Instructions:

1. Take water in a large pan with a lid and add the beans to it. Steam cook the beans for 5 to 7 minutes, until tender. Drain the remaining water. Keep aside.

2. In a pan, add the oil along with the garlic. Stir in the beans until evenly distributed. Heat well for 10 minutes until the beans are well cooked and lightly browned.

3. Season with salt and pepper.

Day 24: Recipe # 47: Avocado Stuffed Turkey Balls

A flexible recipe where you can use any kind of meat, avocado stuffed turkey balls will steal the show every time you serve it.

Ingredients:

- Lean Turkey, 1 pound (ground)
- Garlic Cloves, 6 (roasted; minced)
- Spicy Mustard, 2 tablespoons
- Egg, 1
- Sea Salt, half teaspoon
- Ground Pepper, quarter teaspoon
- Cumin, quarter teaspoon
- Cinnamon, quarter teaspoon
- Cardamom, quarter teaspoon
- Ground Ginger, quarter teaspoon
- Yellow Onion, half (diced)
- Avocado, half (peeled and cut in 16 pieces)
- Olive Oil (extra virgin)

Step-by-Step Instructions:

1. Blend the garlic, mustard, egg, pepper, spices and salt in a food processor.
2. Place the turkey and onions in a mixing bowl and add the puree. Knead the bowl's contents until uniformly blended.
3. Grease a mini muffin pan with the oil and place the turkey mixture in the tins. Indent each ball and place a piece of avocado inside. Gently work the meat around the avocado until properly encased.
4. Heat the oven to 375° and then place the pan in it to bake for 15 to 20 minutes. Once done, transfer the meatballs onto a paper towel.

Recipe # 48: Chicken-Fried Steak with Gravy

Ingredients:

- 1 ½ lbs. Beef cube steak/minute steak

- ¾ cup Almond flour/all-purpose flour

- ¼ tsp. of each (Pepper, garlic powder, onion powder, and mustard seeds)

- Oil for frying

- 1 tsp. Salt

- Gravy base

For Chicken Cream Soup

- 1 ½ cup Chicken broth

- 1 ½ cup Milk

- ½ tsp. Poultry seasoning

- ¼ tsp. Onion and garlic powder each

- ¼ tsp. Parsley, finely chopped

- Salt and pepper

- Dash of paprika

- ¾ cup Flour

Instructions:

1. Heat oil over medium flame.

2. In a reseal able bag, mix the flour, salt, pepper, onion powder, garlic powder, and dry mustard. Shake well.

3. Scour steaks in flour mixture.

4. Fry and flip until you get the desired brownness.

5. Place it on paper-towel lined plate. Keep it hot.

6. For the chicken cream soup, boil the chicken broth, 1/2 cup milk and seasonings for a minute or two. In a separate bowl, add the remaining milk and flour and make a smooth batter. Add this to the broth and stir constantly until mixture boils and thickens. This will make 2 cans of cream chicken soup.

7. Make a gravy base. Use cream chicken soup as a topping for the gravy.

8. Serve steaks along with mashed potatoes and gravy.

Day 25: Recipe # 49: Pineapple Lime Popsicles

Whoever said that you can't treat yourself while you're on a diet has clearly never tried this recipe!

Ingredients:

- Ripe Pineapple, 3 cups (chopped)
- Lime Juice, quarter cup
- Sea Salt, pinch

Step-by-Step Instructions:

1. Combine all ingredients in your blender and run it on high for a minute.
2. Fill popsicle molds with the mixture. Make sure to leave a little space at the top of each so that the mixture can expand.
3. Place the molds in the freezer for 20 to 30 minutes and then put popsicle sticks through.
4. Freeze for at least six hours and then serve.

Recipe # 50: Chicken and Cheese Tostadas

Ingredients:

- 3 cups Chicken, cooked and diced

- 1½ cups Monterey Jack cheese, freshly grated

- 1 Jalapeño finely diced

- 1½ Limes

- 8 Whole-grain 5" to 6" corn tortillas

- 2 tbsp. Water

- 1 tsp. Cumin

- ¼ tsp. Chili powder

- ½ tsp. Salt

- Toppings: Sour cream, avocado and cilantro

Step-by-Step Instructions:

1. Preheat the oven up to 450 degrees F.

2. Combine the chicken, cheese, water, spices, jalapeño and juice of 1 lime in a large bowl.

3. Lay the tortillas out on a large baking sheet, in one even layer. It depends on the baking sheet as to how many batches are made.

4. Evenly distribute the chicken mixture on top of the 8 tortillas and bake for 12-13 minutes until cheese begins to brown.

5. Squeeze the remaining ½ lime on top of the cooked tostadas.

6. Serve warm with sour cream, diced avocado, and cilantro.

Day 26: Recipe # 51: Date Squares

This dessert recipe has been known to be "dreamy" and "heavenly good" as it creates a soft, nutrition-filled dish that you may think twice before sharing.

Ingredients:

- Pitted Dates, 1 pound
- Juice and Zest of One Orange
- Juice of One Lime
- Water, 1 cup
- Vanilla Powder, half teaspoon
- Baking Soda, half teaspoon
- Himalayan Salt, quarter teaspoon

Ingredients for the Crisp

- Almonds, 1.5 cup (sliced and blanched)
- Coconut Flakes, 1 cup (toasted)
- Coconut Flour, 1.25 cup
- Baking Soda, quarter teaspoon
- Cream of Tartar, pinch

- Himalayan Salt, quarter teaspoon
- Coconut Oil, three quarters cup (chilled)

Step-by-Step Instructions:

1. Pre-heat the oven to 350°.
2. Add the first set of ingredients in a saucepan and cook over medium heat for five minutes. Let the resulting mushy, smooth mixture cool on the side.
3. Place all the ingredients of the crisp in your foot processor and process until the mixture is well combined. Refrigerate the mixture for 15-20 minutes.
4. Press a little more than half the mixture onto the bottom of a square baking pan lined with parchment paper. Place the pan in the oven for 8 to 10 minutes or until the crust turns golden brown.
5. Remove the pan from the oven and spread the date mixture on top. Finally, loosely crumble the crisp mixture on top.
6. Put the pan back in the oven and bake for 22-25 minutes.
7. Allow the dessert to cool completely before cutting 16 squares.

Recipe # 52: Baby Calamari with Garlic

Ingredients:

- 1 ½ lbs. of baby squid/calamari with heads, cleaned and pat dried

- 3 tbsp. Olive oil

- 1 Garlic head, minced

- Red pepper flakes to taste

- Sea salt

- Cilantro for garnishing

Step-by-Step Instructions:

1. In a pan, place the olive oil and sauté the calamari (and calamari heads) for 5-7 minutes, turning a few times.

2. Add the minced garlic and pepper. Cook for some more time till garlic becomes golden.

3. Add sea salt and season. Garnish with cilantro and serve.

Day 27: Recipe # 53: Coconut Treat

If you don't feel like cooking much but really want something to appease your sweet tooth, this is it.

Ingredients:

- Coconut Butter, quarter cup
- Unsweetened Coconut Flakes quarter cup
- Berries or Fruits (optional)

Step-by-Step Instructions:

1. Mix all the ingredients and create small balls which you can eat slowly to savor the flavors.

Recipe # 54: Thai Rice

Ingredients:

- 2 cups Brown rice
- 1 tbsp. Coconut oil
- 3 Garlic cloves, minced
- 1 tbsp. Chopped ginger

- 1 tbsp. Soy sauce without MSG

- 1 cup Cilantro, chopped

- Salt

Step-by-Step Instructions:

1. Heat oil in a pan and add the ginger and garlic. Cook until the garlic smell goes away.

2. Add rice and stir so it is evenly coated. Add water, fish sauce, and salt. Reduce heat and simmer for 20 minutes.

3. Once rice is cooked, sprinkle cilantro and taste for seasoning.

4. Serve the warm rice.

Day 28: Recipe # 55: Warm Cinnamon Apples

If you enjoy baked applies, this recipe will allow you to enjoy what you like without harmful sugars like maple.

Ingredients:

- Fuji or Pink Lady Apple, 1
- Coconut Oil, half tablespoon (melted)
- Cinnamon, 1 teaspoon (ground)
- Nutmeg, dash

Step-by-Step Instructions:

1. Peel the apple and cut it in wedges.
2. In a plastic bag, place the apple wedges and the rest of the ingredients. Microwave the bag and its contents for 2 minutes 15 seconds. Make sure to keep a small unzipped hole to allow the apples to breathe.
3. Remove the bag from the microwave carefully and serve the apples hot.

Recipe # 56: Beef with Eggplant Stew

Ingredients:

- 2 tbsp. Olive oil

- 3 lbs. Chuck roast, boneless, cut into 1-inch cube

- 2 cups Beef broth

- 2 cups Eggplant, peeled and diced

- 1 Onion, diced

- 2 cups Carrots, peeled and sliced

- 2 Bay leaves

- 3 Cloves garlic, minced

- 2 tsp. Dried thyme

- 2 tbsp. Flour

- 2 tbsp. Olive oil

- Mashed potatoes - Prepared

- Salt and pepper

Step-by-Step Instructions:

1. In a large pan, heat oil. Add the beef cubes and cook until brown.

2. Add salt, pepper and slow cook.

3. Next, sauté the onion and garlic, until clear. Add flour, bay leaves, thyme and stir well.

4. Transfer the mixture of seasoned beef broth to slow cooker. Cook it for 4 hours on low flame.

5. Use additional olive oil to sauté the eggplant. Cook for 7-8 minutes.

6. Stir eggplant, carrots into the slow cooker and again cook for 2 hours.

7. Serve it over mashed potatoes.

Day 29: Recipe # 57: Raw Brownies

An incredibly healthy alternative to brownies, Brawnies will make you wonder why you hadn't enjoyed whole foods before.

Ingredients:

- Walnuts, 1 cup
- Medjool Dates, 1 cup (pitted)
- Cacao Powder, quarter cup

Step-by-Step Instructions:

1. Throw the walnuts in the food processor until they're crumb-like. Add the rest of the ingredients later.
2. Press the mixture onto a small baking pan and then freeze it for an hour so that it can grow firm.
3. Remove the mixture from the pan and cut into bars.

Recipe # 58: New York Classic Strip Steaks

Ingredients:

- 2 lbs. Strip steaks, (1 1/2-inch thick)

- 1 tbsp. Extra virgin olive oil, divided

- 2 Cloves garlic, lightly crushed

- 1 Lemon, cut into wedges

- ½ tsp. Ground black pepper, divided

Step-by-Step Instructions:

1. Prepare a grill on medium-high heat.

2. Season the steaks with salt and pepper on both sides. Then place the steaks on the grills and cook for 3 minutes.

3. Then rotate the steaks to 90 degrees and cook for 3 minutes more. This will give a nice grill mark.

4. Flip the steaks and repeat this grilling and rotating method until cooked. Check with a thermometer if the steaks have reached 145 degrees F for medium rare. Cook as you desire.

5. Transfer steak to a plate and wait for 5 minutes. Rub with garlic, drizzle with oil and serve with lemon wedges.

Day 30: Recipe # 59: Lemon Bars

If you're more of a tangy dessert lover, lemons bars may be a better choice to follow your meals.

Ingredients:

- Eggs, 3
- Honey, half cup
- Lemon Juice, quarter cup
- Coconut Flour, 2.5 tablespoons
- Lemon Zest, 1 tablespoon (finely grated)
- Salt, pinch

Ingredients for Crust

- Almond Flour, 1 cup
- Almond Butter, quarter cup
- Honey, 1 tablespoon
- Clarified Butter, 1 tablespoon
- Vanilla, 1 teaspoon
- Baking Powder, half teaspoon
- Sea Salt, quarter teaspoon

Step-by-Step Instructions:

1. Pre-heat the oven to 350°. Coat a baking dish with a little butter.
2. Throw the crust's ingredients in a food processor until a 'crumble' forms.
3. Press the crust onto the bottom of the pan and make sure that it's uniform.
4. Prick the crust with a fork and bake it for ten minutes.
5. Throw all the filling ingredients in a food processor
6. Remove the crust from the oven and pour the filling evenly.
7. Bake for 15-20 minutes or until the filling is set.
8. Let the bars cool on a wire rack or in the fridge if you need to further set the filling.

Recipe # 60: Spaghetti Squash Pasta

Ingredients:

- 3 cups Brussels sprouts, trimmed

- 1 Spaghetti squash

- ½ cup Vegetable broth

- 1 Yellow onion, diced

- 2 tsp. Garlic, minced

- ½ tsp. Chili powder

- Salt to taste

Step-by-Step Instructions:

1. Boil the squash in water for 15 minutes.

2. In a separate skillet, add the broth, onions, garlic and Brussels sprouts and cook for 5 minutes.

3. Add the seasonings and spaghetti squash.

4. Cook until broth has dried.

5. Serve hot.

There are many more recipes that you can learn out there. All you need to do is search for the term 'whole food recipes' and you'll come across millions of web pages ready to ensure a variety in your everyday meal plan.

3 Chapter 3: Energizing Breakfast Recipes

Recipe # 1: Balsamic Blueberry Sandwich

Ingredients:

- 2 Gluten free multi-grain bread slices

- ½ cup Fresh blueberries

- 1 ½ tbsp. Maple syrup

- 1 tbsp. Balsamic vinegar

- 2 tbsp. Coconut cream

Step-by-Step Instructions:

1. In a small saucepan, place the blueberries, balsamic vinegar and maple syrup.

2. Cook for 5 minutes and then drain the blueberries and set aside.

3. Layer the blueberries onto one bread slice and coconut cream onto the other.

4. Close the sandwich and grill the bread until light brown. Serve.

Recipe # 2: Eggs with Basil Pesto

Ingredients:

- 12 eggs

- 1 yellow pepper, sliced whole in circles

- 1 red pepper, sliced whole in circles

- Basil Pesto

- Olive Oil

Step-by-Step Instructions:

1. Use a large non-stick skillet and heat over medium heat.

2. Pour in a tablespoon of olive oil into the pan. Add the pepper rings and sauté for 1 minute.

3. Inside the pepper ring, crack and pour one egg and then place the cover on the pan.

4. Sauté the eggs for 2-3 minutes and serve with basil pesto.

Recipe # 3: Smoked Salmon Frittata

Ingredients:

- 3 - 4 oz. smoked salmon, sliced

- 4 large eggs, beaten with some water

- ½ tsp coconut oil or clarified butter/ghee

- Sliced green onions for garnish

Ingredients:

For the green onion sauce

- ½ cup raw cashews

- 1 cup coconut milk

- ½ cup green onion chopped finely

- 1 tbsp. lemon juice

- ½ tsp. Garlic power

- Salt and pepper to taste

Instructions for green onion sauce:

1. Ground the cashews in a blender till it is fine. Add coconut milk, lemon juice, and garlic powder and blend till the mixture is thick and creamy.

2. Add the chopped green onions and season with salt and pepper.

3. Refrigerate to thicken the sauce.

Step-by-Step Instructions:

1. Use a large skillet and add the oil or butter. Evenly coat the pan with oil.

2. Add the beaten eggs now

3. Preheat the broiler.

4. Cook the eggs till the end starts to pull away from the edges and the middle portion is still wet.

5. Now place the skillet under the broiler. Cook until the eggs are set, firm and springy when you touch

6. Now remove the pan from the broiler and slide the eggs into the plate.

7. Top with the sliced smoked salmon, with the chopped green onions. Liberally dress with onion sauce and serve.

Recipe # 4: Crab and Bacon Tacos

Ingredients:

- 4 Slices cooked bacon, crumbled

- 6 Eggs, beaten

- ½ tbsp. Bacon fat reserved

- 6 oz. Crab claw meat, drained

- 2 tbsp. Chives, chopped

- 4 Whole wheat tortillas, warmed

Step-by-Step Instructions:

1. Use a pan and add the bacon fat. Cook the eggs in it and stir often for 2-3 minutes.

2. Add the crab and toss it gently for around 2 more minutes. Add the crumbled bacon as well.

3. Spoon them into tortillas and garnish them with chopped chives before serving.

Recipe # 5: Italian Roasted Chunky Potatoes

Ingredients:

- 2-3 lbs. Organic gold potatoes, cut into large chunks

- 4 tbsp. olive or avocado oil

- 2 tsp. Italian seasoning

- salt to taste

Step-by-Step Instructions:

1. Preheat the oven to 375 degrees.

2. Add all the ingredient and mix them in a large bowl. Pour them into a baking sheet in single layer.

3. Bake the potatoes for 30-35 minutes, until they are tender and golden brown. Serve.

Recipe # 6: Celery Root, Yam with Bacon Hash
Ingredients:

- 6-7 pieces of bacon, diced

- 1 celery root, peeled and cubed (1/2 inch)

- 1 large yam, peeled and cubes (1/2 inch)

- ½ large onion, diced

- 1-2 tbsp. ghee

- 1 tsp. smoked paprika

- 4 cloves garlic, minced

- Sea salt and pepper

- 1-2 tbsp. fresh parsley, minced

Step-by-Step Instructions:

1. Fill a pot with water and add a pinch of salt. Once it boils, add the cubed yams into the water. Cover and cook for 15 minutes till the yams are tender.

2. Once they are cooked, drain the water.

3. In a large sauté pan, cook the bacon pieces till they are crispy. Use a slotted spoon and remove the bacon. Add the onions to the leftover bacon grease and sauté. Cook for 5 minutes till they are translucent.

4. Add the celery roots and cook till they are soft. It may absorb all the bacon grease so you may add the ghee to the mix so that the hash does not burn.

5. Once the celery roots are soft, add yams and garlic and cook till yams turn brown.

6. Season the hash with salt and pepper. Add the smoked paprika and bacon and mix gently.

7. Garnish with the chopped parsley and serve.

Recipe # 7: Kasha Porridge

Ingredients:

- 2 cups Water

- 1 cup Kasha

- 1 stick Cinnamon

- 1 tbsp. Maple syrup

- 1 pinch Salt

Step-by-Step Instructions:

1. In a sauce, add the water and toss the cinnamon stick in. Bring to a boil.

2. Add the kasha and a bit of salt.

3. Reduce heat to low and cook for 15 mins.

4. Serve the porridge with maple syrup.

Recipe # 8: Chicken Tacos with Sweet and Mild Salsa

Ingredients:

- 2 Chicken breast halves, boneless and cooked

- 12 corn Tortillas

- 1 tbsp. Honey

- 1 jar Mild Green Salsa

- ½ cup crumbled Mexican cheese

Step-by-Step Instructions:

1. In a skillet, heat the honey and salsa. Remove half of the salsa into a bowl.

2. Chop the chicken into chunks and add them to the rest of the salsa. Cook on medium heat for 5 minutes.

3. Warm the tortillas in a skillet and place them on plates. Then add 2 tablespoons of the chicken salsa and sprinkle some cheese.

4. Fold the tortillas into half and serve with salsa.

Recipe # 9: Skillet Poached Eggs with Leeks, Pea-Tendrils and Spinach

Ingredients:

- 2 tbsp. olive oil or salted butter

- 2 Eggs

- 2 cups Pea tendrils and spinach leaves

- 1/2 leek, sliced finely into half moons

- Salt to taste

- Freshly ground pepper, to taste

Step-by-Step Instructions:

1. Take a small skillet and heat the butter or oil. Add the leek and sauté for 3-5 minutes till tender.

2. Now toss in the pea tendrils and spinach. Stir well until they wilt and then season with salt and pepper.

3. Take another pan and make a well using the greens. Crack an egg into this well and season well.

4. Cover until the egg is cooked as you desire and serve.

4 Chapter 4: Healthy Lunch Recipes

Recipe # 1: Vegetable Quesadilla

Ingredients:

- Canola oil spray

- 1 cup Spinach leaves, sliced

- ½ cup Bell pepper, diced

- 1 Whole grain tortilla

- ¼ cup Salsa

- ¼ cup Mild Cheddar, shredded

Step-by-Step Instructions:

1. Place a skillet on medium heat and coat it with the cooking spray

2. Add the bell peppers and sauté. Then add the spinach and cook till it is wilted and soft.

3. Push the veggies to one side and place the tortilla into another. Add cheese over half of the tortilla and then place the vegetable on top. Fold in half and cook until the bottom is brown. Carefully flip and cook the other side.

4. Place on cutting board and slice into wedges. Serve with salsa.

Recipe # 2: Chickpea Caesar Salad with Quick Chicken

Ingredients:

- 6 Chicken nuggets, cooked and chopped (leftovers work great)

- 1 Head romaine lettuce, chopped

- ¼ cup Caesar dressing

- 15 oz. Garbanzo beans, drained

Step-by-Step Instructions:

1. Toss all the ingredients into a bowl.

2. Serve.

Recipe # 3: Arugula with Lemon, Steak, and Parmesan

Ingredients:

- 1 bunch Arugula

- 1 ½ lbs. Beef tri-tip

- 3 tbsp. Extra virgin olive oil

- 1 ¼ tbsp. Balsamic vinegar

- 2 ½ tbsp. Lemon juice

- ¾ cup Parmesan cheese, shaved

- Salt and pepper to taste

Step-by-Step Instructions:

1. Combine oil with salt and pepper and keep aside.

2. Grill the beef and let it cool for 10 minutes. Then slice it thinly.

3. In a bowl, toss in the arugula with the dressing. Place the beef slices and top it with parmesan. Serve.

Recipe # 4: Broccoli and Chicken

Ingredients:

- 2 lbs. Chicken, diced

- 7 cups Broccoli, diced

- 2 tbsp. toasted Sesame oil

- 2 tbsp. Ginger, grated

- 1 tsp. Salt

- 1 tsp. Garlic powder

- 1 tsp. Red pepper flakes

- 2/3 cup Coconut aminos

- 1 tbsp. Tapioca starch

Step-by-Step Instructions:

1. Take a large skillet. Put the oil and then toss in the broccoli, ginger, garlic powder, red pepper flakes, coconut aminos, and salt.

2. Cook for a few minutes over medium heat until the broccoli softens a bit.

3. Add the chicken and turn flame to medium- high. Cook until the chicken is cooked, stirring intermittently.

4. Add some tapioca starch and stir well until the sauce is thick.

5. Serve with noodles or cauliflower rice.

Recipe # 5: Lentil and Quinoa Salad with Cashews

Ingredients:

- 1 cup Quinoa

- ½ cup Green lentils, sprouted

- 2 tbsp. Dijon mustard

- 2 tbsp. Bragg liquid aminos

- 2 tbsp. Bragg sprinkle seasoning

- 2 tbsp. Red wine vinegar

- 2 cups Baby arugula

- ½ cup Red bell pepper, roasted and diced

- ¼ cup Cashews, toasted

- 1 Shallot, minced

- 1 Lemon, wedged

- 1 Fennel bulb, thinly sliced

Step-by-Step Instructions:

1. Cook the lentils and quinoa in separate pans, as per directions. Drain lentils and set them aside to cool.

2. In a bowl, add shallot, arugula and fennel bulb and whisk in the amino' s (all of them). Add the lentils, quinoa, and bell peppers, and mix.

3. Garnish with cashews and lemon wedges and serve.

Recipe # 6: Beef and Bone Marrow Soup

Ingredients:

- 1 pack Marrow bones (2-3 pounds)

- 1 pack Grass fed soup bones (2-3 pounds)

- 12 cups chopped vegetables (Use leafy greens, carrots, and rutabaga)

- Filtered water

Step-by-Step Instructions:

1. Place the marrow and soup bones in a large pot. Add the filtered water to the pot.

2. Boil the water and then reduce to simmer for 2-3 hours.

3. While the meat gets cooked, prepare the veggies.

4. When meat is done, remove bones from the broth and add the vegetables to the broth.

5. Cook in low flame for about 30 minutes. While this is cooking, remove meat, tissues and the marrows from the bone.

6. Shred the meat and set aside. Add any fat, marrow or connective tissues to the meat and bones to a blender.

7. Cover this with the broth and blend till smooth.

8. Add meat and the blended tissues to the cooked vegetables.

9. Serve hot.

Recipe # 7: Stuffed Avocado with Garlic Shrimp

Ingredients:

- 2 cups Shrimps (medium to large), raw and frozen - defrost before cooking.

- 1 whole Avocado, medium

- Olive oil

- 5-6 cloves Garlic, minced

- Salt

- Ground pepper

- Fresh parsley, chopped

- Chili powder

Step-by-Step Instructions:

1. Halve the avocado and remove the pit. Also, scrape out most of the meat and leave the shell with a thin layer. Keep aside

2. Chop up the meat and place in a bowl. Crush some with your fingertips. Keep aside.

3. In a medium pan, place 2 tablespoons of olive oil and toss in the minced garlic and shrimps.

4. Add some salt and cook over low heat till the shrimps becomes moist and pink. Don't overcook as it may turn dry and hard.

5. Add the shrimps with the garlic and olive oil into the bowl with the avocado meat.

6. Add the chopped parsley and mix well. Add a pinch of chili powder to get a zing.

7. Now spoon the shrimp and avocado mixture into the avocado shells and garnish with pepper and parsley. Serve.

Recipe # 8: Orange Chicken Stir Fry

Ingredients:

- 2 Chicken breasts, diced

- 2 tbsp. Avocado oil

- 1 tbsp. Tamari soy sauce

- 1 navel Orange, peeled

- 4-5 cloves Garlic, peeled

- 1 tsp Fresh ginger

- ½ tsp. Salt

Step-by-Step Instructions:

1. Take a pan and stir fry the chicken dices in the avocado oil. Add some salt to it.

2. Prepare the orange sauce by blending navel orange with ginger, garlic, and tamari sauce.

3. Once the chicken is tender and brown, add in half of the sauce.

4. Keep stirring until the sauce disappears.

5. Serve with sauce.

Recipe # 9: Creamy Red Curry Slaw

Ingredients:

- 2 cups Broccoli slaw

- ¼ cups Mayonnaise

- 1 tbsp. Thai kitchen red curry paste

- 1 Avocado, diced

- ½ cup Yellow bell pepper. chopped

Step-by-Step Instructions:

1. In a bowl, toss in all the ingredients and serve.

2. You can eat them plain or with rice or in a gluten-free wrap.

5 Chapter 5: Sumptuous Dinner Recipes

Recipe # 1: Sautéed Shrimp and Couscous

Ingredients:

- 1 ½ lb. Shrimp, medium, peeled and deveined

- 8 cups. Baby field greens

- 1 tbsp. Extra virgin olive oil

- 2 cloves Garlic, minced

- 1 ½ tsp. Lemon juice

- 1/3 cup Italian vinaigrette dressing

- 1 ¼ cup Couscous, cooked

- 2 tbsp. Parmesan, grated

- Salt and pepper to taste

Step-by-Step Instructions:

1. Heat the olive oil in a skillet and sauté the shrimp and garlic over medium heat. Add salt and pepper to season them.

2. Cook for 5 minutes until the shrimps are done. Add lemon juice and stir.

3. Arrange the greens in a serving bowl and add the dressing. Toss them. Place the salad on serving plate, add the shrimps, couscous, and some cheese and serve.

Recipe #2: Spaghetti and Meatballs

Ingredients:

- 1 lb. Ground beef

- 2 cups Nomato sauce

- 4 Zucchini

- ½ Spaghetti squash

- 1 Onion, small, finely chopped

- 3 Garlic cloves, minced

- 1 tbsp. Fresh herbs

- 2 tbsp. Butter or Ghee

Instructions:

1. Cook the spaghetti squash and prepare the vegetable noodles. If you spiralize it, add a generous amount of salt and let it sit.

2. Take a bowl and mix the ground beef, garlic, onion and seasonings. Divide the mix into 15 meatballs.

3. Take a large pot and add 2 tablespoons of oil. Add the meatballs and cook them well so the outsides are brown.

4. Add the Nomato sauce and the other desired seasonings.

5. Cover and let it simmer for 10 minutes.

6. In the meantime, rinse the spiralized noodles well. Add the vegetable noodles to the pot and stir well.

7. Check if meatballs are booked and noodles done as per your taste. Serve hot.

8. For separate servings, you can sauté the noodles after rinsing them over medium heat until tender. Serve meatballs on top of noodles.

Recipe # 3: Carrot and Potato Kugel

Ingredients:

- 6 Potatoes, peeled and grated

- 4 Carrots, grated

- 3 Eggs, beaten

- 1 Onion, sliced, minced

- 6 tbsp. Matzo meal

- 2 tbsp. Parsley, chopped

- Canola oil

- 1 ½ tsp. Paprika

- ¾ tsp. Black Pepper

- 1 ¾ tsp. Salt

Step-by-Step Instructions:

1. Preheat the oven to 375-degree F.

2. In a bowl, mix the carrots, potatoes and onion and then add the eggs to the mix.

3. Stir in the Matzo meal, salt, pepper, and parsley and pour the mix into a baking pan that has been greased.

4. Use the entire content, sprinkle the top with paprika.

5. Bake for an hour till they are brown. Serve.

Recipe # 4: Cilantro Lime Halibut

Ingredients:

- 1.5-2 lbs. Halibut

- 1 cup Cilantro

- 2 Limes

- ½ cup Olive oil

- 3 tbsp. Olive oil separately for cooking

- Salt and pepper to taste

Step-by-Step Instructions:

1. Place all the ingredients except the fish and cooking oil in a blender and blend well.

2. Marinate the fish for 10-15 minutes, by placing them in a Ziploc bag and pouring in the cilantro mixture into it. Toss until the fishes are coated well.

3. In a skillet, add the 3 tbsp olive oil on medium heat. Add the halibuts and cook for 4-5 minutes each side. Serve.

Recipe # 5: Tofu and Black Bean Tacos

Ingredients:

- 1 pack Tofu, extra firm, drained

- 1 can Black beans, drained and rinsed

- 1 tbsp. Extra virgin olive oil

- 1 ½ tsp. Chili powder

- ½ tsp. of each (Dried oregano, Ground cumin, Ground coriander, Sea salt)

- 3 Green onions, minced

- 3 Cloves garlic, minced

- 12 Corn Tortillas, warmed

- 3 cups Green leaf lettuce, shredded

- 2 cups chopped tomatoes

- 1 ½ cup Cheddar cheese, shredded

Step-by-Step Instructions:

1. Take a bowl and place the tofu. Mash it with a fork and add the chili powder, cumin, coriander, oregano and salt. Set aside.

2. In a skillet, heat oil and sauté the garlic and two-third green onions for 2 minutes.

3. Add tofu to the skillet and cook for 10 minutes. Stir well.

4. Add the beans and rest of the green onions and stir again for 2 minutes.

5. Spoon the tofu into the tortillas and top with lettuce, tomatoes, and cheese. Serve.

Recipe # 6: Creamy Chicken Salad with Apples and Yogurt

Ingredients:

- 1 lb. Chicken breast, skinless, diced, cooked

- ¾ cup Celery, minced

- 2 Green onions, minced

- 1 Apple, chopped

- 1 cup Cottage cheese

- 2 tsp. Lemon juice

- 1 tsp. Honey

- 1 tsp. Dijon mustard

- 2 tbsp. Plain yogurt

- 2 tbsp. Milk

- Salt and pepper to taste

Step-by-Step Instructions:

1. Place the chicken, celery, green onions and apple in a bowl and keep aside.

2. Put the cheese and all other ingredients in a blender and puree them until they are smooth.

3. Pour this mix on the bowl with chicken and apples and stir gently to coat.

4. Cover and chill until you serve.

Recipe # 7: Tangy Tuna Salad Sandwich

Ingredients:

- 6 slices Whole wheat sandwich bread

- 6 leaves of Butter lettuce

- ¼ cup Yogurt

- ¼ tsp. Curry powder

- 2 tbsp. Green onions, chopped

- ½ tsp. Lemon zest

- 1 tbsp. Dill, minced

- ¼ cup Celery, chopped

- 1 tbsp. Raisins, seedless

- 1 can Tuna

- ¼ tsp. Salt

Step-by-Step Instructions:

1. Combine all the ingredients except for the bread and lettuce leaves and mix well. Refrigerate for half an hour.

2. Spread on the bread and top with lettuce leaves. Serve.

Recipe # 8: Roasted Monkfish and Tomatoes

Ingredients:

- ¾ lb. Monkfish fillets, skinless and boneless (sliced into medallions)

- 3 Roma tomatoes, sliced

- 1 ½ tsp. Extra virgin olive oil

- ½ tsp. Crushed red chili flakes

- ½ tsp Salt

- ¼ tsp. Pepper

Step-by-Step Instructions:

1. Preheat the oven to 450-degree F. Line a baking sheet with some parchment paper.

2. Place the fishes and tomatoes to make two rows, slightly overlapping.

3. Season with salt and pepper and drizzle the olive oil on them.

4. Sprinkle the chili flakes and roast for 10-12 minutes without flipping. Serve.

Recipe # 9: Leg of Lamb with Roasted Fennel

Ingredients:

To Marinade

- ½ cup Orange juice

- 1/3 cup Olive oil

- 1 cup White wine

- 2 Lemon, juice and zest

- 2 Garlic cloves, chopped

- ¼ cup Mediterranean dried seasoning + reserve 1 tsp for gravy

- 2 tsp. Salt

- 6 lb. leg of lamb, boneless and tied

For Gravy

- 3 Fennel bulbs, quartered

- 2 tbsp. Vegetable oil

- ½ cup White wine

- 2 cups Chicken broth

- 2 tbsp. Flour with 2 tbsp. unsalted butter

- Zest from 1 lemon

- Salt and pepper to taste

Step-by-Step Instructions:

For Marinade

1. To make the marinade, take a bowl and place the lamb legs into it.

2. Take the rest of the ingredients for marinade along with salt and pepper and blend into smooth paste.

3. Pour the paste into the lamb bowl and mix well. Refrigerate for a day.

4. When you plan to roast the lamb, take the bowl out and bring it to room temperature before roasting.

For the Roast

1. Preheat the oven to 450 degrees F. Toss the fennel into the oil and then place the fennel into the bottom of roasting pan. Now take the lambs out of the marinade and then place it on the roasting pan.

2. Discard remaining marinade. Pat the roast until it is dry. Brush it with olive oil and season with salt and pepper.

3. Place the lamb with the fat side facing the roasting rack. Roast for 20 minutes. Then reduce temperature to 300 degrees.

4. Roast for another hour and a half and stick in a thermometer to check if the middle portion of the lamb is 145 degrees.

5. Let it cool down for 20 minutes and then carve it and arrange with the roasted fennel on a serving platter.

For the Gravy

1. Heat the roasting pan on medium heat. Then stir in the wine and scrape the bottom of any drippings.

2. Add the chicken broth and the other spices. Then let it simmer for 5 minutes. Whisk in the flour and butter mixture into the gravy and cook for 2 minutes.

3. Add the lemon zest and salt and pepper to taste. Pour on the lamb. Serve hot.

6 Chapter 6: Yummy Snack Recipes

Recipe # 1: Creamy Garlic Broccoli

Ingredients:

- 3 ½ cups Broccoli florets

- ½ cup Creamy garlic hummus

- Black pepper

- Lemon juice to taste

Step-by-Step Instructions:

1. Cook the broccoli florets. You can steam, boil, roast or grill them.

2. Now, in a bowl, toss the florets in garlic hummus and coat them.

3. Add lemon juice and black pepper on top before you serve.

Recipe # 2: Zucchini Hummus

Ingredients:

- 2 Zucchini, medium, peeled and chopped

- ½ cup Tahini

- ⅓ cup Olive oil

- ⅓ cup Lemon juice

- 1½ tsp. Cumin

- 3 Garlic cloves

- Salt and pepper to taste

Step-by-Step Instructions:

1. Combine all the ingredients in a blender and mix them until they are smooth.

2. Serve with crisp raw veggies like celery sticks, cucumber slices, carrots etc.

Recipe # 3: Kale Chips

Ingredients:

- 1 bunch Kale, washed and dried

- 2 tbsp. Olive oil

- Salt to taste

Step-by-Step Instructions:

1. Preheat oven to 300 degrees F.

2. Remove the center stems from the kale and tear or cut the leaves.

3. In a bowl, toss the kale and olive oil together. Sprinkle with salt.

4. On a baking sheet, spread the kale leaves and bake at 300 degrees F for 15 minutes or until crisp.

7 Chapter 7: What to Eat and What to Miss

As is the case with any new diet, you're bound to wonder whether you can have certain foods or simply stick to the ingredients mentioned in this book's 30 recipes. Simply put, your food selection is anything that fits the definition of whole foods – unprocessed and unrefined. This means you can eat meat, seafood, eggs, vegetables, fruits, and good fats such as those found in nuts and seeds.

Foods to Miss

To be even clearer, you need to avoid the following:

- **All Forms of Sugar** – Whether real or artificial, sugar shouldn't be part of your diet. This includes maple syrup, honey and xylitol. Make sure to read labels carefully to avoid consuming any of these by mistake.

- **Alcohol** – Don't consume alcohol or use it for cooking. The same applies to all tobacco products as well.

- **Grains** – Wheat, rye, oats, barley, corn, rice and even gluten-free grains such as quinoa shouldn't be part of your diet. Even products based on these shouldn't be in your home or on your table. So read labels carefully to avail all grain-made foods.

- **Legumes** – Beans, peas, chickpeas, lentils and peanuts are also on the not-to-eat list. Also avoid all forms of soy, including soy sauce, miso, tofu and lecithin.

- **Sulfates** – Sulfates, as well as MSG and carrageenan, should be off your table as they're usually part of processed foods and beverages.

- **All Your Favorite Comfort Foods** – Bread, tortillas, muffins, French fries, biscuits, chips, caffeine and all the other edibles you love and add to your weight should be out of your system for the next 30 days.

If you're confused about any edible, simply leave it for the next 30 days. Whole food recipes are abundant, ensuring sufficient diversity to appease your palate. And, no, the program won't starve you. Instead, it'll help you lose weight and gain the strength required to be active in life.

Limit Yourself

The 30-Day Whole Food program isn't as strict as you may think. You can have the following in moderate amounts.

- **Fruit Juice** – You can have fruit juice and use it to sweeten some desserts or recipes. However, make sure to either squeeze it fresh yourself or.
- **Clarified Butter** – Unlike traditional plain butter, clarified butter is allowed in this diet. For starters, it doesn't contain protein. Therefore, it won't affect the program or go against your efforts to lose weight.
- **Fava Beans** – You can have GREEN fava beans only. This is because they aren't legumes just yet, but rather pods. And, no, regular fava beans are off the table for you.
- **Vinegar** – You can take your pick from white, balsamic, rice, apple cider or red wine. However, steer away from malt vinegars and other varieties that contain added sugar. These contain gluten and can harm your health as well as affect your diet.

- **Salt** – Despite iodized salt containing sugar, you can have a little bit of salt in your diet. Your body needs some sugar in order to function and metabolize food and nutrients effectively. Therefore, don't deprive it from a limited dose through salt.

One last tip: don't try recreating baked goods or treats with any of the approved ingredients. A pancake is always a pancake no matter how healthy its ingredients are. If you fail to remember this particular tip, you might as well leave the program altogether. Mixing old food with whole food recipes can be even more dangerous, so make sure to swear these off for the next 30 days.

The Not-Permitted Food List

1. Vegetables: Potatoes

2. Grains: White, polished grains, rye, barley, wheat, and oats

3. Proteins: Processed meat

4. Dairy: Cheese, unclarified butter, margarine, cow/goat milk

5. Seeds and nuts: Peanuts

6. Flavorings: MSG, soy sauce, artificial fruit essence, malt vinegar

The Permitted Food-List

1. Salads and vegetables (non-starchy)

2. Whole fresh fruits (except bananas) and fruit that is canned or bottled without sugar.

3. Lean meat that includes poultry, duck, turkey, chicken, reduced-fat bacon like turkey bacon, lean ham, and reduced-fat sausages.

4. Egg whites

5. Fish, shrimps, crabs, prawns, beef, elk, buffalo, mutton, veal, turkey, soy

6. Reduced-fat cheese (chiefly cottage cheese)

7. Tea, coffee, and low-calorie juices

8. Seeds and nuts like almonds, walnuts, pistachios, pecans, pumpkin seeds, sunflower seeds, flax seeds.

9. Grain include millet, quinoa, corn, buckwheat and brown rice

10. Fats include olive oil, ghee, and coconut oil

11. Flavorings include maple syrup, herbs, spices, balsamic vinegar, apple cider vinegar, red wine vinegar, honey

12. Daily include rice milk, almond milk, coconut milk, clarified butter and free range eggs.

8 Chapter 8: Recommendations to Get the Most out of the 30-Day Whole Food program

While controlling what you eat is 80% of the 30-Day Whole Food program, it's hard to ignore the fact that discipline, an active lifestyle, and healthier lifestyle changes are necessary. Therefore, to ensure that you achieve great results once the 30-day period is over, here are some valuable recommendations you should build your life around.

#1) Take the Time to Plan Your Day

Planning beforehand will help you avoid events where cheating on your whole foods diet are inevitable. For instance, planning your day knowing that you have a meeting at 2pm will allow you to plan your breakfast and lunch at times when you'd feel most satiated and less likely to binge.

You'll also need to plan what you eat every day. That way, you won't be overwhelmed by the large number of whole food-based recipes out there. Besides, you'll know what to expect when you get home, avoiding the temptation of junk food. You can plan your whole week in advance using the following as an example.

#2) Stop Calories Counting and Checking Your Weight

By embracing a whole foods based diet, you can forget about counting calories ever again. The ingredients used in making the dishes are very weight loss-friendly, which means that they won't be adding inches to your waist. In fact, the reduced calories in these will allow you to burn more calories and grow leaner quickly.

As your body will be experiencing changes during the next 30 days, you shouldn't check your body's measurements or your weight. If you don't see results, you may decide against continuing this regimen. However, everyone reacts differently to this change of diet. Some tend to lose weight after ten days while others start from the very first day. The best time to take your measurements and weigh yourself is before starting the 30-Day Whole Food program and once you're done with your first thirty. And, yes, there will be more because of this program's great results.

#3) Embrace Healthier Habits

Aside from what you eat, your stress levels, hormonal imbalance and other effects of unhealthy habits will take their toll on your body, adding to its mass. By sleeping for at least six hours a day, you can allow your body to effectively metabolize food and control hormones which the brain produces and can cause weight gain. Similarly, controlling your alcohol consumption and drinking more water will keep you hydrated, therefore less likely to eat more later. You can ask your physician or dietician for more guidance and techniques to complement your new healthy diet.

#4) Don't Forget to Exercise

A diet based on whole foods will help you lose weight, but exercise is what you need to keep it off and shape up. Exercise will further help you survive the upcoming 30 days, especially if you take up meditation or yoga to achieve peace of mind and grow more patients. However, make sure to select the best exercise for you at the moment. For instance, if you're too overweight, consider water aerobics since they don't put much stress on your joints. On the other hand, slightly overweight individuals can start off with weight training and move their way towards aerobics.

#5) NEVER EVER Cheat

The essence of the 30-Day Whole Food program is to make good food choices regardless of the situation. So never cheat over the span of 30 days. Doing so will reverse everything you've done, forcing you to start from the beginning once again.

Never make excuses out of special occasions. This is where you need to show persistence for entire 30 days, and this is how your abstinence will be tested. If you eat inflammatory foods, even in a small amount, your hard work will be ruined. A single pizza bite or a tiny amount of milk in your coffee is enough to breach your healing cycle. So become committed to the program, recipes, and these five recommendations.

9 Conclusion

Now that you have a good idea of what you're up against, you may be worried about not making it through. However, the fact that you decided to purchase this particular book means that you're ready to lead a healthier life where you're both physically and mentally fit. Therefore, have no fear and be more confident about yourself.

Again, thank you so much for trusting me to guide you through your weight loss journey. I hope that everything you read and decide to follow helps you lose weight and grow fit in the future.

If you found this book worth reading, please leave a review on Amazon so that others can purchase it too and reap the same benefits you will very soon.

Thanks for everything; have a great time! - Edwards Adams

Made in the USA
Middletown, DE
08 May 2016